FRED

After the famous portrait by Norman Manwaring

DRAGONKIND

The Song of Lament of the Lord Dragon
Federigo il Barbarossa
(Fred)
Michael Francis McCarthy

THYLACINE PRESS
2007

First Published

THYLACINE PRESS
8 Little Surrey Street
DARLINGHURST NSW 2011
email: thylacinepress@bigpond.com
Website: www.thylacinepress.com
ABN: 91 641 984 498

Previous works:
 An Armorial of the Hierarchy of the Catholic Church in Australia 1998
 Heraldica Collegii Cardinalium
  Volume I 1800 to 2000 2000
  Volume II 1198 to 1799 2003
  Supplement I (for the Consistory of 2001)   2003
  Supplement II (for the Consistory of 2003) 2005
Armoria Sedium 2001
A Manual of Ecclesiastical Heraldry, Catholic, Anglican, Lutheran and Orthodox 2005.
Armoria Pontificalium, A roll of Papal Arms 1012-2006 2007

National Library of Australia
in-publishing entry:

McCarthy, Michael Francis
 Dragonkind

 Fantasy

ISBN 978-0-9577947-8-8

Because of Hugh

From his birthday in the Midday Sun

And because of the inspiration of those dragon artists who have gone before, especially Norman Manwaring whose drawing of a dragon published in the work The Heraldic Imagination by Rodney Dennys was the initial genus of Fred. Also Stuart Devlin for his rendition of the Frilled Lizard on the Australian two cent coin; J R R Tolkien for Smaug, Francis I of France for his Salamander and Styria for it's panther. Finally I am grateful for the myths and legends of the ancient and medieval worlds, even if I have mangled them a little along the way.

Michael McCarthy, 25th March 2007.

*The question is always the same with a dragon, will he talk to you or will he eat you? If you can count on the former ....why then you are a **DRAGONLORD***

Ursula Le Guin, Earthsea

DRAGONS

I, FEDERIGO il BARBARROSSA, Lord Dragon of the Antipodes, second of the Council of the Nine......._Crave your attendance, to listen anew to the saddest of songs, the Lament of a Dragon, in the shadow of his power, a force no more._

All Dragons are of a time of before, a time no longer revealed, and all that is true is hidden. Names being sources of power, power that is no longer ablaze, are true and therefore likewise hidden, in hope of better times that will not now, alas, come. Out of the Light of the true, Dragons use lesser names to protect that which is theirs with their waning strength. For myself the title of a newly dead King was taken: dead for defying and denying that which was and is true, that power which has waned. Consumed of the FLAME, his name stands as a warning to those who do not believe.

Sages will tell of me much that is true, much that is merited, but will deny me the place I am due. In all things much can be foretold and events can be directed to the ultimate goal, but

3

always the unexpected can, at the worst possible moment, alter for ever the best determined courses and purposes. So it was with me; and I must say in truth also with us.

At a time of great peril, I and another, who should have heeded the course of events and prevented the gamble of the reckless, dallied in a tryst, all being lost, and all for her.

Beauty without peer, spark from the FLAME, a fire ablaze in the morning's cold glory. Ah, the memory of her..........

ESMARELDA, the Portuguese Strumpet, beloved but perfidious, loved but not loving, promising.....

but always evasive, failing in that which destiny demanded. Seeing her still as if in the mists of a dream, she draws me thither, against all my strength, to desire....that the unrequited might be made full.

Choosing at last, as all Dragons do but once, she chose not me, the light of the world, but him, the sixth lord.........

4

UMBERTO the Treacherous,
the Terror of Thrace,
beloved of her......

to be as one in tomorrow's dreams. He, that guarded the limits of the Councils powers, distracted by that which was deemed and destined as mine, failed to perceive or acknowledge the danger, the folly of us all; and he should have done.

At the moment of peril, seeking his council, I sought him, amidst the thundering of the drums of doom, in the place of his wisdom, but alas, to no avail.......

Turning then, powerless, I saw them, locked in the dance of the Flame..,

a fire lighting the heavens. All was lost: all that might have been would now come to naught. For myself the way would be alone.....for us all, not at all.

9

But I forget myself: this all came about at the end of our time. The beginning demands...the beginning was....was, the **COUNCIL OF THE NINE.**

Dragons are beings of the Flame, forged by him at the beginning of time, and all that they are and do is ruled by it; birth, death and infinity.

For the governing of this he called into being the Council, to be of a plenium of Nine, that was to be kept even beyond the falling of its individual members.

The council was ruled by ....

KRACKON, the first of the Nine, wise to the last, never forsaking his name......

His strength always the power of the Flame. Because of this oneness he will endure when all else is extinguished. He, for this reason, was entrusted with the burden of maintaining the plenium of the Nine.

11

Many were considered, but only eight could be chosen. Of these was I second, chosen to keep the History of it all, that the truth of it might endure. Of Umberto, the Governor of the limits of the power you already know.

Next considered was.....

Cedric of Wales, a God dispossessed, sulking and skulking in the mists of Powys......

lamenting the loss of his sway. But being more interested in the ruling of men, than in the service of the Flame, he turned away and faded into the folds of the fabric of time, from whence the illusion of power still seemed to persist.

12

Next there was chosen......

Daud of Pesidia, third of the Nine, guardian of all wisdom, keeper of the Dragon law......

splendid and proud, this noblest of Dragons, whilst serving the Flame,never once stooped to its pleasure, always seeking a higher plane.

15

Elected then, out of place , for fulfilling of his function was........

Ezbra, the scourge of Numidia, last of the Nine, harbinger of death and desolation......

that he might sweep clean those places and demons who would not serve, as serve all now must.

Not elected was........

SMAUG, the despair of RHÛN,
avaricious beyong measure,
noted by authors,
chronicled for his end

.....despised for himself, even by others of dragonkind; He that lives on piles of gold eventually becomes of it, glittering, hard and cold.

Came there then elected....

Sandro of strompboli, protector of the flame, fourth of the nine, eternal keeper of the secrets of the dance, deep in his volcanic cauldrons......

that each in his time might know, perceive, understand and achieve. To our sorrow, with time his knowledge of the darkness dimmed and the instinct for danger dulled.

With him, the lord of life was chosen.........

Ombalic, Lord of the Northern waste, the eighth lord, nightsinger to the world, singer of the song of songs of the sorrow of sorrows, the knowledge of death.......

death come at last in the dark void of despair. Dragons do not perceive of death, and except it not gladly...But then you do not know of these things...You should, for without it much will remain unclear.

Dragons live and die in their destined way....follow me as I show its lay.......

the way of the Flame, of fire and thunder. Of the Flame, by the flame and through the Flame is the path of all Dragons, time to no end, shrouded as it is from all by the swirling of mist, the breath of us all.

Birth, from an egg, forged in the flame, to the strength of completeness

.....emerging whole into the circle of the FLAME, to be nurtured by it but briefly, Dragons knowing no childhood, to be fully with it in but an instant.

Death, always at the Hand of the Titan, the dark side of Man..........

for dragons do not die of themselves, but merely fade and fade..... For from the beginning have been such as GEORGE the dragonslayer, who would not and could not understand. Being not of the FLAME, and heeding it not, using the powers of dark ignorance they prevailed but seldom, but when prevail they did, Death came to a dragon and the fabric of the FLAME was rent, wavering in the firmament for an instant.

At such a time, when all seemed desolate, the way of renewal of the infinity of the Dragon spirit came anew.

29

INFINITY,
reborn from the fruit of the Flame,
come forth in the fullness of time

31

carried as it is by she,

from the dance of the flame, the spark of life

when out of love would come the seed to conquer anew the sorrow and disperse the bitterness of defeat.

33

That all might know of such tidings of sorrow and renewal is sent

ELIALIAL, the messenger, wraith wandering in the dark, listening without rest......

for the assent to the way, this symbol of the working of infinity.

Thus live and die Dragons, and these Lords govern its way

Elected next for his magnificence was

....HAN NUN, Lord dragon of the Orient, fifth of the nine, most successful of dragons, holding sway in his diadem almost to eternity....

but not quite.

Eternity being endless, not even his strength could prevail all the way. In truth, all followings are in the ultimate feckless, and the longer they are held, the more crushing is their defection, and when time is full, nothing alters the passing of a dragon's strength, not fury nor cunning; not even the power of the FLAME.

And sadly even the source of life, the FLAME itself, can be perverted to dark paths and purposes, as was tried by

The BASILICK, the demon of death, accursed of dragonkind, taunted by the sting of its innocence in its tail

a final punishment for his transgressions.

Granted the seventh siege of the nine, he sought to pervert the power held jointly to himself, wishing for the power of all the nine. In this he was secretly encouraged by the Titans, the Demons and the Fell of the Dark. Seeking a disguise for his convenience, he, like all schemers, was exposed whilst betwixt and between, and being caught vulnerable, was caste out and punished with his torment....That evil can face all with impunity, but the perpetual vision of its own innocence, never reattainable, haunts for all eternity.

At this time there was also driven out

The COCKATRICE, pale shadow of the last, less in venom, less in guilt, exiled in perpetuum to Siberia's pale

there to do good works, that he might expiate his service to and imitation of he who had utterly fallen.

Krakon, in his wisdom, sought first to replace the fallen with

41

The HYDRA,
born of a wanton who danced of the Flame
more than but once....

43

to the confusion of many and the malforming of the way. He did this to show that Dragons except all equally for themselves, even if they do possess many heads filled with small brains......but she would have none of it in any of them. Haughtily she proclaimed that as she had been born apart, she would walk apart. Her delusions lead her on a bizarre path, ending as it did, defending the fleece of a sheep at the gates at the end of the world from the darkest of the Titans, Jason the Argonaught.

Next was there considered

the SALMANDER, of the flame but less than it, transfixed in its sway....

for want of its secret......and there krakon left her. Some power had she however, and this she did use in the service of a Frankish king, many being singed because of it.

45

Finally was there chosen

AUSTRALIS, the frilled, elected for his meekness, seventh of the nine, in lieu of the accursed....

Sadly more of a mascot than a master, his presence, not to mention his prescience, did not add strength to the council, and in time of peril this error was costly, and cost dearly.

FOR THE DRAGON ELECT THERE WERE BUT TWO REALITIES, DRAGONS AND DRAGONS DREAMING ....TO DREAM, SO GREAT A GIFT, SO DEADLY A DANGER.

Given by Him, through the power of the FLAME, that for the use of others, nature might be conjured to others paths, as need seemed to decree. Warning did he infer, that only in fullest knowledge should this be proceeded with and then only to the limit of need. Those with reason were not in the brief, and interference there would cost dearly. How quickly pride forgets peril, for pride there is in success and overweening pride in failure to succeed.

DRAGONS DREAMING

Dreaming first.......

of the OPINICUS, the proto griffin, for the keeping of treasure dreamt.....

for an eastern king's treasure house door. Soft and gentle, with a voice like honey, none passed him by, seduced as they were by its charm to turn away. Both he and his treasure are now gone, he to his peace and the treasure to the dust of time.

Of SEBASTIAN the mailed, perverse and perverted, a warning ignored....

thirsting for that beyond his retinue, driven as if addicted, he crossed beyond that which he could hold and perished, in pain, withered to nothing, deprived as he was of an avenue of return.

Of the GRIFFIN,
given to ARMENIA for her protection,
lingering still on Ararat....

perplexed by the non presence of his charges. They went long ago, whilst he dallied with the things of time.

Guardians are all very well but they must be ever vigilant, nothing can hold back that which will be for ever.

Of the Unicorn, champion of the virginal, precursor of she who rode on the moon, foretold by a star....

the hope of Mankind but not of Dragonkind, foretelling as it did of a time beyond our fall when hope would come anew.

Of PEGASUS, the flying stallion, born out of the Gorgon's end, proof of light to the lost.....

that even out of the greatest evil good can ensue. But alas, not all that begins well continues so, and thus with him, falling as he did under the sway of the Titans, the enemies of us all. It was now becoming apparent to us all that all created beings would not be controlled and whilst those that are benign would do no harm, others would be otherwise.

Of the PANTHER of Styria, not of the flame but dragonlike, a deadly error....

for here was one not benign, who saw herself as a rival of us all. Imprisoned in a mountain cavern, she rages still causing, from times to time, snow and rock to plunge from its slopes.

61

Pondering on the error, we dreamed of

the TYGRE, the Seer, haunted to the last by a vision of its future perceived......

But here the balance was too inlooking and the poor paranoid creature, foreseeing the whole of tomorrow, feared for itself and pined to nothing.

Reality seemed to demand more than this.

Interrupted from this ponderence of nature of light and dark by promises of assistance we dreamed ......

Of the WINGED LION, Champion of the messenger, guardian of the way......

for his chosen against the demons of the dark.....

Of the QUESTING BEAST,
conjured for **PELINOR,**
to his eternal loss…..

loving it as he did to distraction, loosing sight of his own kind forever......

Of the winged STAG of Gaul, timid and despairing of the arrow.......

leading the gentle to the pastures of peace, but sadly even for Mankind this time has still to come.

Returning then to the problem, the puzzle that beset us, in hope of besting the evil shadow we dreamt of ....

the fabulous PHEONIX, reborn from the flame to lead anew those who had fallen.....

but being from beyond the flame, she retreated into the wilderness to be at one with it, to serve neither us or them. This answer did not satisfy.

Indeed the notion that the answer lay in isolation and retreat was beyond belief; that our fruit would want us not offended deeply. This could not be the answer.

Distracted for the last time we played with a new realm, the vastness of the oceans. To rule it we dreamed ...

of HORSES of the sea...then....now.....

of the UNICORN, committed to the sea, but with the gift of flight...and....

of the terrible twins, lions of the sea, piscine and serpentine, lost in the gleam of the others eye.

But of course none of these ruled in the domain, being distracted by their inner selves which remained of the land. They drifted for awhile then mutated or faded and were lost to us. Too late did we remember that others ruled the seas.

The final dream of joy was ...

OF SHE THAT LIVES IN NESS,
allusive and mischievous,
bane of saints and sinners alike…

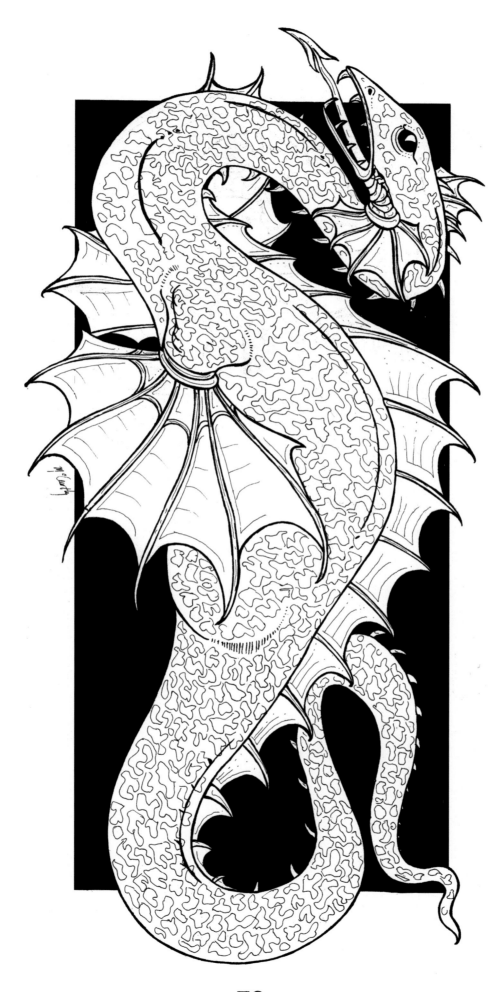

79

the joy of joyless times, a child of better days.

Returning finally to the ultimate, we dreamed again of the pusslement and dreamt ...

of the Serpent Eagle, a dream distorted, the ultimate evil, crushed only by the absolute will of the nine...

Evil now seemed to lurk in all our dreams, the world would not do our will. Pride in our destiny demanded a final solution, that we might by our wills rule all. Then was suggested by SANDRO the ultimate peril, and many dissented. Debate was endless, back and forth, to do or not to do. I fearing the worst sought the advice of him who was absent, whose duty it was to prevent such excursions beyond our limits.

81

But unfortunately UMBERTO was busy, as you will recall. The result was tragedy. Distraught, I ceased to care, and assented. As UMBERTO was absent his role was ignored. And so we dreamed

Of LOHENGRIN, the man made swan..

and this to prove that nothing was beyond us.

RETRIBUTION WAS SWIFT: dragons dream no more.....Dragons rule no more, we merely are.

THE NINE LINGER STILL, SPECTRES FROM THE PAST, WATCHING NOW WITH DREAD HINDSIGHT, THE PATH OF THE NEW DREAMERS.........

MANKIND.